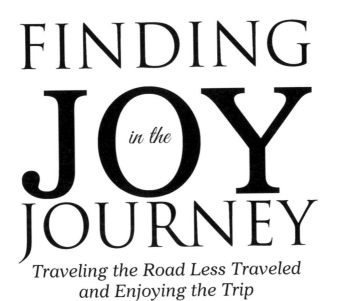

FINDING
JOY *in the*
JOURNEY

*Traveling the Road Less Traveled
and Enjoying the Trip*

Anne Joy

WESTBOW
PRESS®
A DIVISION OF THOMAS NELSON
& ZONDERVAN

WestBow Press books may be ordered through booksellers or by contacting:

WestBow Press
A Division of Thomas Nelson & Zondervan
1663 Liberty Drive
Bloomington, IN 47403
www.westbowpress.com
1 (866) 928-1240

ISBN: 978-1-4908-8599-5 (sc)
ISBN: 978-1-4908-8601-5 (hc)
ISBN: 978-1-4908-8600-8 (e)

Library of Congress Control Number: 2015910171

Print information available on the last page.

WestBow Press rev. date: 08/04/2015

Contents

Prologue

Finding JOY in the JOurneY
Traveling the Road Less Traveled
and Enjoying the Trip

O NE OF LIFE'S MAJOR MILESTONES is graduating from high school and then deciding from there which path to choose; whether to continue on to pursue a degree at a community college or university, go directly into a job, or travel the world.

This is an exciting time in life's journey now that you are moving from the routine of spending time in a classroom setting to learning to be out in the world, on your own, and making your own decisions.

When one comes to the end of their life, they might be asked, as the saying goes, "what did you do with your dash?" The "dash" is the time between the year you were born and the year of your death.

Instead of looking back at what cannot be changed, re-phrase this saying to, "what are you going to do with your dash now", to set the course for the rest of your dash?

Now that you are in the position to be making decisions for your future and more in control of your "day to day", what can you do to fill in the dash to make the most of every day and enhance the journey you are about to embark on.

Now that you are leaving high school to move into higher education, a job, into a technical school, or possibly you have obtained your degree, and you are already leaving college to go into the work place. What will you do with your dash now?

Some will find their journey taking them into the age of ninety or more and for some, life's journey will be much too short.

Your journey through life is unique to you. Will you be controlled by things, such as playing video games, having five thousand friends on a social network, texting, checking your text messages while you sit with friends at a restaurant, talking on your cell phone, cruising the mall, surfing the Internet on your cell phone, watching television, or will you be in control, and living life to the fullest and really experience finding the joy in the journey of life?

Included in the following chapters are some ideas to make the next phase of your journey, wherever that takes you, more fun, fulfilling and fruitful and tips for you to build on using your own unique skills and talents that you have developed to this point. Tips to help you put tools in your toolbox.

You will be able to adapt the ideas in the following chapters to your unique personality and lifestyle.

The hope is that these will stretch you, so that you will enjoy daily situations and opportunities that are on your path, rather than coasting through life, or being overwhelmed when life coasts over you. You will develop the tools in your toolbox at hand to use. Your path is unique to you as an individual.

So whether you are reading this as a new graduate or if it has been years since you achieved that milestone, we all have a dash, so I hope what you will experience here will enhance what you experience in your own personal and unique dash.

Focus On It

NOW THAT YOU HAVE GRADUATED and determined where you are headed, whether it is moving into a university dorm, your own apartment, or a new job, learn to focus on today. You will find if you work on this, it will enhance your days and what is going on around you. You will learn to savor what is happening around you in the today you are experiencing.

Planning for your future is important, but in twenty- four hours, today will be over, so it is important to learn to focus on what is happening in your today to make the most of each day you experience. At the end of the week, you will have accomplished more because you will have gotten the most out of each day.

Too much time is spent focused on what is going to happen later in the week or what has happened in the past. If you spend time complaining at the beginning of every week that it is not already Friday, how much will you get out of every Monday, and the rest of the week? Not much.

There are seven days in each week that should be fully enjoyed. This is your one time passing through this life, and wishing on every Monday that it was already Friday, robs you of living in the moment and fully experiencing what is happening on Monday, Tuesday, Wednesday or Thursday, because the focus is that the only important day in the week is the one before the weekend.

Learn to focus on what is going on around you at the moment in the current day, instead of wasting today thinking about things that happened in the past that you cannot change or about a future planned event or a day that has not yet arrived.

Even though a day is measured as having twenty –four hours, if you take into account the part of each day that it takes for you to rest (as you should, because rest from sleep is important in order to function fully), you really have less than twenty-four hours each day to impact your dash and then the day is past. So maximize your time every day!

Focus on what you can derive from the time in the present day. Money invested over time can draw interest and grow which is beneficial, but time is like water flowing behind you going over a waterfall if you are paddling a canoe in the opposite direction; it is behind you and gone.

If you have already invested the years to get an undergraduate or master's degree and have found employment within the field for which you spent years training, then be glad when it is Monday, and you are where you are.

You have already succeeded in a couple of areas: choosing your career path, doing the necessary work to get there, and successfully finding employment in the field you chose.

If you are just finishing high school and are now embarking on a career path or moving into your first year of college, this is the best opportunity to make those days count.

You are in the best position to take the time to research what is going to work to get you to where you want to go, but enjoy living in each day that you are working toward that goal.

Initiate and cultivate, don't alienate. The days of "cliques" should be over for you now. Try to initiate conversation with a wide range of people whose paths you cross in your day, including those with whom you work or go to class. This will provide opportunities for you to learn and grow while accumulating various points of view and ideas; as well as potentially developing new friendships.

Friendships made during the post-high school years often last a lifetime and are one of life's treasures.

Focus on Preparing

Preparation can save time and money, so preparing is a good skill to acquire.

Whether it is a doctor appointment, getting to a sporting event or movie on time, arriving on time for a flight, or just meeting friends, being late is an annoyance for you and the person who is waiting. Recognizing the importance of being prepared and being on time will pay off in your career, as well as in your leisure time.

Being late to catch a flight or to arrive at port for a cruise could possibly cost you not only extra money, but could potentially cause you to miss a much anticipated vacation. Making the effort to be on time will take focus and planning, but is easy to accomplish and will pay off with a valuable tool to add to your toolbox.

If you are starting out as a freshman at university, start by being on time for class. If already on a job, make the effort to be on time for work each day and focus on being early for business or department meetings.

Utilize a day planner in whatever form that works best for you.

Arriving on time for work is a key to surviving in the work place. Arrive consistently late and you could be a target for dismissal. Arriving on time will go a long way in making a great impression as you show reliability and dependability and choosing to arrive early is even more impressive and may work to your advantage in the long run.

Making this a priority when you are just starting out in your career or while you are at university will be a tool that will become a habit and serve you well and is an easy habit to acquire.

Buying an alarm clock is an inexpensive purchase, but also alarms are often included in the features of your cell phone.

If your main alarm is a favorite clock radio that uses electricity, be sure that your backup alarm is one that uses batteries or one you have set on your cell phone. By using multiple alarms you have a backup if you forget to set one or if the power to one fails.

Often cell phones have an alarm feature that gives you the flexibility to set multiple alarms for different times such as weekdays or weekends. By using multiple alarms, you should never have to suffer the embarrassment of arriving late to work or class due to the fact that you overslept. Organize your morning routine to maximize time for sleep and also so you waste less time getting ready in the morning. Anything that you can do the night before to organize and save time in the morning will be valuable in making your morning less rushed. Getting in the routine of choosing what clothes you plan to wear, having presentations or class materials organized and ready will make the process of getting ready to go in the morning much smoother.

With such a wide variety of breakfast foods and juices available, it should be easy to find something healthy and nutritious to prepare and eat in the morning, so that you do not have to sacrifice having breakfast. An option if you prefer, is to wait to have breakfast once you get to work. This could be a good strategy, as often getting out the door earlier helps you beat rush-hour traffic.

Some work places have a kitchen, cafeteria or deli in the building and you may find that there are co-workers who would like to join you in the morning for coffee and breakfast before starting your day. Whether preparing something to eat at home or at work, incorporate breakfast into your morning routine. Be creative; be healthy.

Since it is also important to be prepared and not to run out of gas on the way into work or class, incorporate into your schedule the best time of day to stop to fill up your car if you drive yourself to work or to a location where you then take public transportation. If it works better, pick an evening during the week to fill up or make this a task to have done before the end of the weekend.

Practice preparation in the area of all of your appointments and this will start becoming a habit, making it effortless for you to be on time. Preparing will be a tool that will serve you well in helping to stay on top of appointments and important meetings.

Whenever making an appointment, notate the appointment time in your day planner or calendar as being ten minutes earlier than actually scheduled. Although you cannot count on being seen sooner, sometimes arriving earlier does work to your advantage. Either way, it is better to be early than to have to stress about being late.

As an example, for a 4:00 appointment, note on your calendar to arrive at 3:50 with the attitude that if it is an appointment to see a physician for example, you might possibly have a long wait. The time now that you are spending waiting can be wasted time or it can be productive time. You could spend the time texting and occupying the time with your phone. Preferably, you will be more creative and prepare ahead how to use this time productively by bringing something with you to occupy the period of time that you have no control over.

You might consider subscribing to a magazine that provides an opportunity for you to use this time to read and learn about a subject that interests you or a subject you want to learn about. You might consider a yearly subscription; change each year to a new magazine and keep this in your car for doctor's appointments or when you are waiting in any situation, such as having your vehicle serviced.

Waiting in doctor's offices or at the mechanic's will be a small part of your week, but use the occasions when you are waiting to take a break from your devices. This can be a time to stretch your mind rather than texting, posting to social media or surfing the Internet.

You may also discover when you do this often enough, that now the time spent waiting is not wasted time because what you learn from being productive during the waiting is a gain in your knowledge that will stay with you and may pay off at some future time.

You can also take steps that might help make your wait shorter. If possible, try to schedule the first appointment of the day or the first appointment after lunch.

Often, two or three patients are scheduled for the same time slot. Arriving early to the appointment often puts you ahead of the others. It is much better to arrive on time, plan for delays, and be prepared with something to occupy your time. Then the whole experience won't be as frustrating.

There will be occasions when, even with your best preparation, circumstances warrant leaving and rescheduling. Decide how long you will wait past the time of your appointment. If you feel that the circumstances warrant it, advise that you would prefer to come back at another time when the doctor is running more on schedule. You may even decide that this person does not run his or her practice in a way that you can afford to sit and wait an extended amount of time at every appointment. This is something that you have to make a determination about. You have to weigh reasonably being patient and when the amount of time that you find yourself waiting is unacceptable. If you are uncomfortable with the way things are going, then by all means, you may just want to leave if it's not a critical appointment that must be done right away and try finding another doctor. Don't let anyone tell you that you owe for the visit. You did show up for your appointment on time. Advise that you have been waiting "x" amount of time past your appointment time and that you will contact them later to reschedule. Whether or not you decide to do that is up to you. You may find another doctor who is able to run the practice in a more efficient way that you like better. You have the right to this flexibility. Being prepared to be on time and having something to occupy your time, will make the process of waiting in any kind of setting less stressful and more productive.

Focus On Maximizing

Evaluate your college courses to be sure you are maximizing your position to get the most out of the classes you are taking. If you have a dream to be an opera singer would it also be wise to think about a double major into something that will pay the bills while you wait for your break onto the Broadway stage after graduation. Always take advantage of direction from faculty advisors to be certain you are not taking any courses unnecessarily and you are on the right path with your schedule of classes to move into your career choice.

If you have already begun your career, evaluate your career position to maximize what you are getting for what you are giving. Evaluate the benefits. Does your employer provide health care insurance, short term and long term insurance, life insurance, paid vacations and retirement savings plans to help you save towards your future retirement?

Do you feel led to start your own company or do you have an idea that you think would be successful.

Don't waste time getting by in a job that is easy, but is not providing you with benefits. Health emergencies can cause a great deal of financial hardship. Investigate opportunities to obtain further education or training to continue to enhance your skill set so that you have better opportunities in the job market that afford you not only an income, but afford you benefits as well.

Many waste opportunities because they don't want to take the time to be informed of what is available. Many waste taking advantage of investing in a 401k with an employer match which over the years equates to money lost if you don't enroll and take advantage of this benefit.

If someone suggests a position that intrigues you that you had never thought of before, find out what additional schooling you would need and determine if it is something worth pursuing. If you feel that you have the skills that will afford you the opportunity to travel abroad and find work along the way, focus on maximizing this time to do the traveling if this is your dream. Don't let excuses interfere and lose focus and put off something that you want to do and can do now because it will be devastating years down the road to look back and say to yourself, "I wish I had …." Woulda, shoulda, coulda is not where you want to be. Instead you want to be in the "Did Zone".

If just beginning a teaching career, consider now moving forward with getting your master's degree through evening classes. Although it may take a little longer, ultimately you will have the advanced degree in a few more years; while continuing to earn income. This will also put you in a position to earn a higher income once you have completed your master's.

Focus on maximizing the position you are in at university and in your career. Maximize opportunities that present themselves to you now that could help you in your future.

Focus on Balancing Responsibilities and Leisure Time

With all the stresses and responsibilities you have, try to schedule time to do things for yourself that are relaxing to help balance out the stressful times of your day. Different forms of relaxation appeal to different people. Find your niche and strive to find a good work/play balance. Working a fifty to sixty hour work week is necessary in some professions, and for some periods of time, to get ahead, in those professions. In other situations, it is good for the employers; particularly if you are salaried and putting in the extra hours for the same pay you receive for forty hours.

Evaluate where you are and focus on finding the best balance for your situation.

Refer to Focus on Preparing. The "rush hour" does not have to the "rush hour" for you if you plan to arrive at work ten to fifteen minutes sooner than you are scheduled. You will have a much better reputation around the office being on time, or even early, than running in late every day. Also, the fact that you are taking the initiative to arrive early may be noticed around the office and pay off when it comes time for lateral moves to positions with more potential or for a promotion.

An additional benefit to focusing on punctuality is that it will, in fact, slow you down as you are not rushing around in a panic five days a week trying to beat the clock and get to work on time. Your pace in the morning will be more relaxed since you have figured the time you need to get ready and out the door, plus taken into account traffic issues and delays you might encounter along the way.

If you find that you work in an environment that allows for flexibility with your work schedule you may also benefit from arriving early to be able to leave earlier at the end of the day. This may be advantageous as you might beat the "rush hour" traffic; giving you more time for your after work plans.

Whether you drive yourself or take public transportation, you can also make the most of this time as well. You may have a commute through a beautiful area in your community or you may see a beautiful sunrise every morning that others don't. Use this time to notice the scenery around you. You will be able to use this time to notice things around you that would be missed or crowded out of your mind if you were running late as you would be focused on looking at the time, riding the bumper of the car in front of you and fuming at the red lights that are taking so long to turn.

Having time to reflect on the commute without rushing may bring to mind an idea that might help you in your job or you might problem solve a difficulty that is going on at work and come up with a solution.

Try to follow the same exercise when shopping, as slowing down and giving yourself plenty of time to shop will probably give you the opportunity to calculate the best buy when deliberating about size choices on grocery items for example. You may notice new items you have not tried before and bargains you would have missed if you are in a rush to get in and out of the store due to time constraints. This is not to suggest that you impulse buy or overspend on products you don't need. By taking time to evaluate your purchases, you may find products that work better than what you have been buying in a rush or products that work just as well for you at less cost. It's preferable to leave the store with more of your money in your wallet for the next time it will be needed than leaving it behind due to overspending and wasting money.

Try to organize your class schedule as much as possible and study time needed for your classes so that you do have time to enjoy the many social activities that you don't want to miss.

If you find that you have a good balance with class, study time and time for social activities and time left over, it may be worthwhile to consider looking into a part-time job to start building a reserve account.

There are many options for wise investing. If your schedule allows for a part-time job to start bringing in income while working on your degree start investing part of this now for future needs. This is a great choice if you are able to manage this with your class schedule and study time.

If you take time off in the summer months from classes, you may want to take this opportunity to take on additional work in the summer to build up your investments and savings or earn additional money to pay down the expenses of college as you go so that you don't have a large debt when you graduate.

If you are already in a career like the teaching profession, you might want to consider using the holiday periods to vacation and the summer months to work an additional job to have money for additional income to start investing for future needs and wants.

The possibilities are endless because you are evaluating your situation, your goals and putting your creativity in place to maximize time where extra work can be a benefit. Having a goal to make the most of your time in your twenties to work as many hours you are able with your schedule to build up savings and investments will pay off so that you can cut back in your thirties, forties and fifties and enjoy the funds you have put away.

Incorporating leisure in your schedule to replenish and refresh is also essential.

Exercise in Action

This is a very simple exercise, but one that will have lasting positive results for your lifetime. This is an exercise that will help tremendously so that you will enjoy each day, you will learn to focus on the present, not live in the past and not be in the habit of yearning for a day ahead of where you are at the moment.

Mark off a thirty-one day period on your calendar and create a journal. For the next thirty-one day period, focus on the events of the day and make brief notes at the end of each day of what you did in the day. Make notes of things you notice in the day that you might have missed if you weren't making a conscious effort to focus only on today's events. Opportunities that you pay attention to today, often end up having an effect on your future, so these are opportunities in the present that you don't want to miss.

During this same period organize your schedule to arrive early to appointments, to class or work. Once you have worked on this exercise for a period of thirty-one days, this should become part of your routine so that you will find it easy to plan when you have to be somewhere at a certain time and get there on time without effort.

Notice the difference it makes in allowing you to slow down the pace and how much more relaxed you will be by making the effort to take the steps to be prepared to be on time.

At the end of the thirty-one days, read your complete journal. When you read back you will see how much you have accomplished by staying focused in each day, on the day, and how making the effort to arrange your schedule to be on time relieves the stress of the consequences of being late.

At the end of this first exercise, you will have a couple of new tools in your tool box

Count It

A S YOU LEARN TO FOCUS on each day to get the most out of your day, also look for hidden blessings in each day. You will discover hidden blessings in the day when you look for them. You will most likely discover that even though you may find yourself in trying circumstances on some days, by learning to count your daily blessings, you realize they don't stop.

This is not to minimize when one experiences tragedy in their life. Any tragedy experienced leaves one reeling to make sense of what has happened and it is a process to work through recovering from any tragedy. So this chapter is more about looking for positives even in the trying circumstances and working on the ability to look for blessings hidden while walking through the problems that come at you.

Be accountable that you are not creating the trying circumstance. Don't shoot yourself in the foot by not considering the consequences beforehand when making decisions. Recognize that your actions create circumstances which can be detrimental to you and/or someone else.

Don't blame the consequences that result from poor judgment on bad luck when they are nothing more than the result of poor judgment.

If you don't spend the time to research a purchase such as a car or house and overspend, or research a way to offset costs for living expenses and education expenses, then the resulting level of debt is there due to the lack of taking time to evaluate and research options.

Count on waiting as an option. Make today count, but today might not be the day, when what you want is going to happen. Count on having delays. Count on having to possibly wait, but this might turn out to be a blessing.

Blessings that come after patience and forethought have been put into the equation are often the most treasured blessings because you were not able to see them as such at first, but had the situation turned out differently and the way you wanted originally, it would not have been as fulfilling as the way it turned out in the long run.

This will make much more sense to you after you once experience it for yourself. Being receptive by exercising your mind to be open is the key. Digging your heels in that there can only be one solution or outcome and it can only turn out the way you had it originally planned is living in futility and often unhappiness.

Exercise in Action

Create the chart below for yourself for a period of thirty-one days. Write down five blessings that you notice as you go through your day.

Whenever I eat strawberry shortcake, I think what a blessing; that God made such a delicious fruit and what a blessing that someone thought of whipped cream in a can and shortcake.

At the end of the exercise, you will find that when re-reading the blessings you have listed, you will see blessings that you would have overlooked before. You will find that you will have a more positive outlook about walking through situations that you would rather not be in.

When these situations happen, your mind will be more open to find solutions to "move the mountain" that may be in the way of your goals. Often, going around the "mountain" to look at the problem from a different perspective for a different solution than you had previously considered is a better outcome for you. However, you won't see that it is a possibility unless you are more open to count blessings that at first seem like negative situations, but after a season of time, prove to have been a blessing in disguise.

Day 1 -Date	1.
	2.
	3.
	4.
	5.
Day 2 - Date	1.
	2.
	3.
	4.
	5.

Frame It

FRAME YOUR DAY BY PUTTING others as the center of the picture and you behind the camera as the photographer. In your interactions with people who you come in contact with in each day, look for opportunities where you might do something for someone else.

When you step back and notice things that you can do for someone else, it can be as simple as making eye contact when passing someone and smiling, letting someone go ahead of you in line at the store, letting someone out in front of you in traffic. Even while driving, if someone cuts you off, resist the urge to retaliate and just let it go.

You might have the opportunity to help a co-worker with a project where there is no benefit to you, or consider helping another student in a subject in which you are gifted and they are struggling. Tutoring in a subject you are accomplished in to help a fellow student could also bring in extra income for you. You may overhear in the checkout line that someone is short on change and offer the money to help them.

When you're looking for a parking space at the mall or anywhere you are shopping, take the focus off of your need and think how fortunate you are to be able to drive to the mall. If you are healthy and able to walk, then park your car farther out and walk. You may be leaving the closer space for someone who really needs it more than you. You will be walking quite a distance once you are in the mall or store anyway, so why make a big deal of it if you cannot find a parking space close to the entrance and you have to park a little farther out. If you plan on most of the time doing just that and if you are fortunate that you turn the corner and you do find an empty space – great. Once you get used to this, however you might find yourself passing up the spaces closest to the door leaving the space for someone who needs it more than you.

It is a challenge to put the wants and, sometimes needs, of others before your own. However, it is a good exercise to practice. Not only to take the focus off of yourself, and practice also noticing what is going on with others around you. Instead of being oblivious to your surroundings, it will open you up to see what is happening and possibly give you the opportunity to do what only you can do.

Focus on and enjoy the moments as you progress through the day and notice when you encounter someone else in the same space in time in your day with a need that is unexpected. When that happens, be especially focused on what you might be able to bring to the table to meet the need. Since there is no one else like you, what you have to contribute can be important and significant to others, no matter how small or insignificant you think it may be. Your actions speak volumes about your personality and character.

Envision a picture of the kind of day you are going to have where you not only look at what you can get out of the day, but what you can give to others you encounter in that day. This, of course, does not mean to put yourself and your safety at risk at any time or to put yourself in a position to be taken advantage of.

The years that you are in college or university will be such a rich opportunity to practice this because you are in a setting where you will be meeting different people in each class that you take, club that you join, sorority or fraternity that you become a part of, or part-time job you might decide to take while going to university. In addition to the fellow students that you come in contact with, you will also have interactions with the faculty and staff. Just by being conscious of shifting the focus off of yourself - to open yourself up to look past yourself - to what is happening with others you encounter each day affords you additional learning experiences and will enrich your day.

If you are attending college or university in a town away from home, make the most of this time to get involved in some aspect of on and off campus activities while you are there for this period of time since you will likely move on from that location after graduation. Explore opportunities for part-time work in town after class or on the weekend. This will expose you to even more relationships and opportunities for learning on the job as well as in the classroom and involve you in off-campus experiences.

If you are entering the job market right out of high school, you have the option to look into opportunities to take an occasional evening class, to explore other opportunities to learn with training offered by your employer while you are working and broaden your experience and relationships.

Look for opportunities at work to get to know co-workers and supervisors in other departments. Be open to explore opportunities within the organization in other offices in other cities that may take you further in your career. Be available; to volunteer; to help. Even if it seems like you are giving and not being compensated, you will usually find a reward in the giving of yourself at some point.

If you have an opportunity at your place of work to participate in a volunteer activity in the community take advantage of this opportunity to spend a few hours giving of yourself and benefiting someone in need. This may also give you the chance to participate in something you have never experienced before such as volunteering to participate in a telethon where you would help take calls from others giving donations, or volunteering to participate in a walk or run that an organization is doing to raise money. If you bowl or play golf, often this talent can be useful not only for your personal enjoyment, but many organizations raise money by having bowling or golf tournaments.

We all have bills to pay and financial responsibilities and don't necessarily appreciate it when we see a panhandler asking for a handout when we have worked hard to earn the money we have. However, look for an alternative way of thinking by focusing on the blessing you can be because you have the good fortune to not be in that position. Determine an amount of money you feel comfortable giving. The next time you buy fast food, purchase a few of the $1.00 "bucks" or food coupons that are sold in fast food restaurants, which can be used to purchase food items from the $1.00 menu. Have these available; maybe in the glove compartment of your car for example, and they will be there when you see a need.

By giving a struggling person a couple of paper "bucks" from a fast food chain, they can have a meal, you have helped, and most likely you will be on your way to a bed to sleep in with a roof over your head for the night and by crossing your path, you have made something better in their day.

Can you offer to help someone with directions or provide a ride to work if someone needs to leave their car to be repaired during a work day? Can you offer to pick up lunch for a co-worker who is working overtime to finish a project? Saving them the time to go out and pick up lunch would even help.

It also could be as simple as noticing a person who is not happy and offering a kind word, to not getting angry when someone cuts you off in traffic or rides your bumper when clearly not only do you have someone in front of you and are going as fast as you can, but you are also planning to turn left at the next intersection.

It will be interesting to see where this shift in focus to others takes you with your interactions with friends and co-workers to people whose names you will never know.

Exercise in Action

Create the following chart. Starting tomorrow and for the next five weeks fill in each day the encounters you have where you observed a need and what you chose to do about it.

At the end of the five weeks, read back over all the things you did and the number of people you encountered where you and the decisions you made, made the difference in that person's day.

Date	What I did for someone else today

Pay particular attention to the fact that those who have received your kindness or assistance absolutely would not have received it otherwise, except for the fact that you took the initiative. The ideas are totally original and unique because they are yours and you will encounter many opportunities in your day. What you decide to do is your idea put into action and the result of your idea and the resulting action on your part to help will benefit a lot of people.

Once you have completed the exercise and look back on what you have done, evaluate how it made you feel to see all of the things you did that made a difference for someone else.

Have you participated in something in the period of the last five weeks that you have never done before because you saw an opportunity to volunteer your time to help?

After you have completed this exercise it is now time to move on to blend it.

Blend It

THERE CAN BE A GREAT deal of frustration and time wasted if one leaves to go on vacation just to turn around a few miles out wondering if they put the garage door down, arrives at a hotel and finds one of the articles that had been carried on the plane didn't make it off or gets to work and wonders if they remembered to turn off the coffee pot.

There is a solution to help remember and to take care of all these examples and more.

To remember something, the trick is to create a "blend".

"I want to remember to…..
unplug my iron when I leave in the morning for class or work"
fill up the car before it gets to empty"
turn off the stove or coffee pot before I leave the house"
know at all times where my house and car keys are"
and to remember not to lock them in the car"
turn off the stove when I finish cooking"

"to easily find where I parked my car in an unfamiliar parking lot"
"remember not to leave sweaters or umbrellas at the restaurant, movie or event."

To blend it so that doing these things becomes a "blend" of motions and habit will take between twenty-one to thirty-one days using the method you decide on. Your "blend" will become a habit of motions and part of your daily routine, saving you lots of time and frustration once you have mastered your "blend", because you will accomplish what you want to accomplish without having to stop and think about it or take extra time. You will have incorporated it into your daily routine; using your creativity and choices of how you set up each blend.

This is a great tool if you are now moving from home to live in a dorm or apartment with other students where you are now taking on more responsibility for taking care of your own living space and organizing yourself for your class schedule and getting to class.

A blend is also especially helpful for situations where you question yourself wondering whether or not, in your haste, you remembered to do something such as putting the garage door down before you drove off or unplugging the iron. It is also frustrating to arrive at class with what you needed to bring still back in your dorm or apartment.

Using this as a tool through your years at university will easily transition into a tool you will carry with you to be more organized when you move into whatever field you have chosen and simplifies many things in your everyday routine.

An example is Cheryl who uses a "blend" in the morning when getting ready for work. She has found a way to combine two things she doesn't want to forget into one "blend".

She irons her clothes in the morning and also uses a curling iron, and wants to be certain that both are unplugged before she leaves for work. She has created a "blend" so that she is sure that both are unplugged and then she doesn't question herself again about it once she's at work; concerned that she has left either on at home.

Cheryl wears a watch every day; so she chose her "blend" to be that she does not put her watch on her wrist until she has first checked to see that the iron and curling iron are unplugged before she puts on her earrings and jewelry.

She keeps her watch in a jewelry case on her dresser. From this location, she can see both the curling iron and the iron on top of the ironing board, so it is just a matter of glancing at both while she puts her watch on to check that she unplugged both. Then she puts on her watch. Using the curling iron, ironing her clothes and wearing her watch are things that are part of her morning routine anyway, so it does not require extra effort for her to use this "blend" as a tool to set up a sequence of not putting on her watch until she is sure she has unplugged what she needs to for safety. If she questions herself on the way to work, she has her answer on her wrist. The watch would not be there if she had forgotten to unplug the iron and the curling iron.

The way this is mastered in Cheryl's case is that Cheryl knows she prefers to wear a watch on a daily basis and she finds it easy to incorporate this with making sure she will not remove her watch from the jewelry case until she has completed checking the iron and curling iron, putting on whatever jewelry she has chosen for the day. Then she puts the watch on her wrist. She is going to do this anyway, so putting on the watch after she checks her curling iron and iron is not taking extra time, she just incorporates it into her routine. This actually saves her time because she gets in the flow of doing this so she doesn't back track re-checking to be sure she has unplugged these things. She knows she has.

Steve, James, and Rick share a house off campus. They have decided to keep their car and house keys on an inexpensive key holder that Rick installed inside the pantry door in the kitchen.

Rick suggested that they use this to create two blends for the goals of - first - not losing or forgetting where their keys are and – second - making sure that the coffee pot, stove and toaster oven are turned off (or unplugged) before they leave the house for class.

This plan works in their case because the key rack for the house and car keys is located in the same area as the appliances they want to be sure are turned off before they leave their home. They know where the car keys and house keys are because they have created a "blend" that they hang their car and house keys on the key holder in the pantry.

The keys do not go in their pockets and they are not thrown on a table anywhere in their house.

If you do not have a pantry, there are other options for establishing a place where your keys will be kept in order not to have the frustration of being in a hurry to leave, and not knowing where your keys are. A basket on a table or drawer that you choose can serve the same purpose as long as this is the only place the keys are left consistently – in the same place.

You will need to create additional "blends" for when you are out in order not to lock the keys in the car or misplace your keys when you are at work, the theatre, or the amusement park for example. You just have to decide what process is going to work for you and once you have mastered this it makes things so much easier than spending time hunting for missing car and house keys or calling for help to get your car unlocked, because the keys are inside the car.

There have been instances where a quick trip to the store has been disastrous when something was left cooking on the stove and somehow caught on fire. Imagine coming home from a quick trip out to pick up something from the store to find your house in flames.

It has happened, because being in a hurry, both thought the other had turned off the stove before they went out the door. Imagine if you live in an apartment or condo where a fire would also affect someone else or cause loss of life for someone who was home while you're out at the store.

Rick's "blend" for remembering to turn off or unplug the coffee pot, stove etc. on the way out in the morning is that before removing the keys from the holder in the pantry, they make sure first that everything is off. Their "blend" is that the car keys are not removed to leave for work in the morning until the appliances are turned off or unplugged.

The use of a simple thing like a key rack or basket and habitually putting the keys only at that location works for cell phones and all the remotes you have. Get creative. Buy an inexpensive basket, tray, or pick a drawer, but create your "blend" that the basket or tray or drawer is where you always go to put the item so that you don't leave it laying around instead.

Remember to include a "blend" so that you don't forget and leave the cell phone in the tray or basket when you leave the house and need it. This can easily be added into the coffee pot "blend" where the cell phone is with you before you get the car keys to walk out the door.

Once you get the hang of the process of the "blend" you will see over time how effortless it is to incorporate into your routine and how much time it saves.

You will find ways to put important papers in a certain area so that nothing is misplaced. Bills can be put in one basket and the due dates written on a calendar. It's as easy as thinking of a process and making the process "blend" in with your routine.

You will not miss your train home because you are searching all over at work for where you set your car keys that you need in order to be able drive home from the station or looking for your phone that you set down somewhere.

Tweak the process as you go along. Give yourself more time if necessary. You may create a "blend" and once you've tried it a few days, you may find a better way of doing things. You may be able to incorporate an additional task. You will succeed and it's nice when your "blend" falls into place and saves you time.

Refer back to the list at the beginning of this chapter and you may find that you have enough ideas to create "blends" to last you for a period of a year or more. Not everything has to be done at once. You may want to start with one idea and when this is achieved, move on to more.

Once you have created and accomplished the "blends" that work for you, you will be ahead of the game on saving time and lots of headaches. You will not be questioning whether you put the garage door down, where your papers are for the big meeting, what happened to the airplane tickets or tickets for the show you've been looking forward to for six months. You won't be trying to pry through the car window with a coat hanger to unlock your car because you left the keys in the ignition or on the seat.

Another idea is to create a "blend" for when you travel with your laptop or go to a restaurant or movie with a sweater, coat or umbrella. Airports have hundreds of articles in lost and found because of things left behind on the plane or going through security. If you create a "blend" for what you take in with you, to the theater, restaurant, plane or train, then you won't be without anything when you leave.

To remember where you parked at an amusement park (where often you are directed and have no choice where you park) use your cell phone or digital camera to take a picture of the row number.

To remember where you left your car for your normal shopping trips pick an area to park and stick with that area.

Park your car forward as often as possible so you don't have to back up when leaving your parking space. This minimizes the times you may come close to backing up into a pedestrian or oncoming car or backing up into someone who is also leaving at the same time. By finding an area where you can pull forward into a space, it will be much easier when leaving than having to back out of the space.

There have been extremes with terrible consequences where creating a "blend" would have been a lifesaver. It is hard to believe, but parents have actually forgotten and left their children in a car seat in a hot car all day; with terrible consequences. Another example is school bus drivers finding children left on their buses. Of course, situations like these are extreme, but once you have gotten used to creating "blends" for the everyday tasks to make your life easier, you will automatically start recognizing ways you can create "blends" for safety as well.

The ways you can create "blends" are limitless and using your own creativity to accomplish everyday tasks is fun and will pay off over your lifetime in saving time, money and frustration.

Exercise in Action

Below is a chart to get you started. You can duplicate this on your computer. Make a list of three goals and then create the "blends" to accomplish them that will work best for you and your schedule.

Give yourself at least thirty days and you should have these accomplished in that time.

You will see after the first "blend" is accomplished and you use it without effort, how much time and aggravation you save and you will get hooked thinking up more and more "blends". It will pay off many times over with the amount of time you would have spent retracing steps or losing things.

Goal	Blend to accomplish goal

D'accumulate

Pick one day a month and make a note on your calendar for the next six months to sort and pitch – "d'accumulate" – things you have accumulated that you do not need that are "cluttering your crib". If there are old bills stacking up, buy a shredder, shred them and recycle the paper. If there's a pair of shoes that you aren't wearing because they kill your feet or you're tired of them, drop them off at a clothes drop or donation center in your area.

To take it a step further, use an empty cardboard box and put things in it that you see on a daily basis that you know you just don't need or use anymore. Drop these things into the box during the rest of the month so that you will be a step ahead on your "d'accumulation day".

You will find that it will make you more conscious of "things" that are accumulating that are no longer valuable and your living space will be more enjoyable to be in. Plus, you will be disposing of things that are no longer of use to you, but can be used by someone else rather than sitting unused and collecting dust.

Exercise in Action

Make a note on your calendar – one day in each month - that you will spend just twenty minutes cleaning out a room, closet or drawer and throwing away, recycling or donating unneeded items.

Change It

C HANGE HAPPENS ON A DAILY basis. Change is inevitable. Don't be averse to change – embrace it because it will happen. Instead of working against the change, go with the change. Work with change and you won't spend so much energy trying to undo what cannot be undone.

Try to look at the situation that has changed from multiple angles instead of negatively or with "blinders on". Whether it's a breakup in a relationship or a change at work that you did not see coming, write down five things that you can do with this change to turn this experience into a positive outcome for yourself. Understanding that you cannot change another person or control some situations that you find yourself in, you can control yourself. You can control your response and your attitude. To control the way you are reacting to the situation and to turn it around for a positive outcome instead of a negative outcome – if possible.

Wasting your time trying to undo what has changed, is wasting your life because you cannot undo what has changed. Your life is too important to waste.

Not every relationship will be successful and result in the conclusion you might have anticipated. That does not mean the experience was a total failure. In the case of a breakup in a dating relationship, although painful and it will truly take time to work through the pain, think of what you might have gained from the relationship.

During this relationship you may have taken away a learning experience from it that will serve you well in the next one. Did you see something in that person that you want to avoid in the next relationship? Although going through this is definitely painful now, try to remember that there was a time when that person was not in your life. Focus now on ideas of where you can meet others to begin a new relationship. Focus on the now and the new start. The water has already gone over the waterfall. What's ahead for you just around the next bend in the road that you don't want to miss? Don't spend any time looking in the rear view mirror.

Have you ever seen a toddler fall and start to cry? Not so much because they are hurt, but because of the suddenness of the shock of falling. Have you ever seen that same toddler in the midst of crying stop immediately if the parent suddenly brought out an ice cream cone? The falling is over; let's move on to the ice cream. Keep your eyes open for the blessing in the change. Most of the time, you will find it over and over again when you look for it.

Examples of things you can do to meet others – be the organizer of a group function with your friends, find a part-time job that will put you in a position to meet guys/girls in your age group in an area that interests you, volunteer in a situation where you can help and learn something, but where you also meet others your age.

Being a volunteer at Special Olympics or at a sporting venue in your area that helps persons with disabilities participate in sports is a great place to fill a need in your community. You may have a special ability to coach or knowledge that could help someone else in this area, and at the same time, be around other volunteers, where there's the potential to meet people who have an interest like yourself.

Don't let discouragement take control. Discouragement can take control in any situation and prevent healing and moving forward to a solution. In the face of discouragement, think of it as "courage" in between two opposing forces squeezing you in.

DisCOURAGEment

You will find a solution when you are focused on using COURAGE in the face of disappointment and not letting discouragement take over your emotions and control the situation. You are capable of finding a solution and making the changes needed to resolve the circumstance in your life. Capable includes the word ABLE. Notice that able is at the end of the word. There is nothing holding the able back and hemming it in. You are able. The future is out there for you and you have the last word on how you handle dealing with the change.

The future is open and waiting for you and there will be a solution leading you to a better future and situation.

Failing to use your courage and being stuck in discouragement is like the word COURAGE being hemmed in the word discouragement. Nowhere to go; it's just sitting there.

Put this into practice by using the following exercise when change happens that you're not expecting and that you don't welcome.

Write down the change and then brainstorm to try to see five ways you can tackle the change you are facing. This should help you to focus on the positives.

In the case of a career change or job loss, this can definitely be a hard process to walk through. When one door closes, actually a far bigger and better door can be opening, but it is hard to walk through the much bigger and better door if you are still turned toward the door that has closed. Focused on the closed door, you miss being focused and moving toward another opening door.

You need to be moving toward the bigger and better door. Walking toward the door and looking for the key to get to it and unlock it is going to take some thought and problem solving. The benefits might not be immediate, but keep focusing on what you can do to embrace the change that has occurred and look forward to moving on to a beneficial outcome.

Exercise in Action

Work on the following exercise for the next sixty-day period. When something changes for you in what appears to be negative way, write it down and look for at least five ways to handle it in a positive way. At the end of sixty days review your results. Has one of the five ideas been the solution? Has progress been made or is this going to take longer to reach a conclusion? With time go back and review to see if by adapting and problem solving if the outcome that resulted from the change that happened was better with time because of your patience, persistence and courage to work through the situation in a positive way. Then you are on a path for the rest of your life to have another tool for your toolbox to help you roll with the punches and handle change.

Situation that has changed:	Solutions to address this change:

Expect It

JUST AS RECOGNIZING THAT THERE will be constant change in your life, you can also expect that your wants and desires won't always go the way you had things planned. There is also Murphy's Law and life happens.

By "expecting it", that circumstances will come along and interfere with your best laid plans, you will be in a better position to deal with whatever life throws at you.

The flexible sail handles the wind blowing into it and moves the boat along on its course. The same wind will knock over the stiff board, that is inflexible, and lay it flat.

Worry will rob you of the things you can learn on the journey. Worry, worry, worry, worry. It's a non-progressive, stagnating thing. Carrying worry around with you is like carrying a heavy weight, which bogs you down. It is definitely not a tool for your tool box. It will not help you accomplish anything.

You don't accomplish a thing carrying worry around. So dump worry and replace it with tools that will help you figure out the solution to whatever problem you are facing. Tools like hope, vision, creativity, and prayer are tools of action which need to replace worry if it tries to take up residence in your life.

Like a bad headache, you are going to take a remedy for your worry and get rid of it. You are going to remedy it with thinking of alternatives and developing problem solving skills. You will be using your creativity and vision, while looking at the situation as an opportunity to stretch. The problem is not going to control you if you control worry.

The path that your life is on is not straight and narrow. Life's path has curves and splits where you must choose which route to take.

Just like a roundabout built in a road, that splits to go around an obstacle in the road, and then you end up back on the same road once you get past the obstacle that the roundabout is going around, you will run into obstacles on your path also. However, once you come around the obstacle, you may have an improved path.

You may have put in the years and effort for the education and then not land in the job you expected. It may not be easy and it could take a lot of time and effort to land the job that is the best fit for you.

Look at the situation you are facing from another angle or use prayer to ask for guidance on what you believe is the right decision.

Example: John's goal is to move up the corporate ladder with his company. Last week, a co-worker was chosen to fill a position with the company that John had hoped to move into next. Is a possible solution going to be to worry and ask now what? Get angry or upset and quit? These are not solutions. These are reactions.

No doubt John has to deal with the disappointment and what he considers a setback. However, now he has the option to put the wheels in motion; to look at other options for the next step in his career path.

Even though he believes he was more than qualified for the position and is not being used to his full potential, he still likes the company. He also like his co-workers, his boss, and the salary is acceptable. So for the time being, he may consider staying where he is and wait for another opportunity with the same company. He may decide to be patient and wait for another opportunity, or he may consider scheduling a meeting with his supervisor to see if there is more potential for advancement for him in another area of the company.

The meeting will be much more productive with John having the most positive outlook and attitude.

The solution to the problem could be that John is not happy where he is, feels that he needs a higher salary now and needs to be in a position where there is more of a challenge.

This is an example of a problem that John did not cause, but he feels he needs to solve because he needs a more challenging position to grow. He also feels he deserves more income for the experience he has.

Patience is one of the tools John is going to use from his tool box to take the time to determine the best solution to move forward for the best outcome.

You may have been in a family growing up where alcohol, physical abuse or drugs was the problem solving tool used when life interfered with expectations. What about the problems and challenges which are self-inflicted? Alcohol and drug use, irresponsibility with finances, egocentric or prideful behavior.

At this time in life, it is time to take on the responsibility of your own decisions and move into adulthood, leaving relying on parents for anything behind. Some adult children feel that when they find themselves with a problem, they can run back home for a solution, but now is the time to move past that. You can expect it, that there are consequences when you make decisions that you know from the beginning are not wise. You can expect it that you are going to encounter challenges and problems in life that, as an adult, you are going to have to learn to solve on your own. Now is the time in life to start taking on this responsibility and learning that you do have the tools to meet the challenges you will face.

Many times, when one doesn't expect it and life throws one into a tailspin, for some it is too much and the solution is to end the pain and their life. For those who choose this route, the dash is over with that one decision. There is no chance to gather the tools in the tool box; to try to fix the problem.

This is the most unfortunate and tragic resolution of any situation. To feel that there is no solution and lose all hope to try to move beyond the situation. To never, ever, know what could have been. To never, ever, know that there was a victory over the circumstances had the time and effort and courage been taken to find it.

Expecting life to throw things at you that you don't like and being willing to deal with this when it happens and go to your toolbox to pull out the resources you need, practiced overtime, you will find that you have stepped it up a notch and added another tool of experience to put in your toolbox.

By working on acquiring tools to deal with problems, and looking at problems from many sides, you will be better equipped for finding possibilities and a better outcome.

When problems land at your feet, it can never be stated often enough that a solution to one problem can often be found while tackling another. It is often in how you approach solving your problems. Becoming an unstressed-out problem-solver is a skill you can achieve.

You have probably heard the adage "this too shall pass" but learn to also turn the meaning of this adage into, this means "the feeling of being overwhelmed shall pass"; not that all problems shall pass.

By believing that the feelings you are currently experiencing of being overwhelmed will pass with the effort of looking for solutions, you may obtain a gold nugget of experience in finding the solution that you can cash in at a future date, when a similar problem comes along.

The other side of the coin is that being flexible when an expectation is not met might be a blessing, but you are so focused on the disappointment, you don't recognize it as that until later.

Exercise in Action

The exercise for the next thirty days is to record any disappointment, problem or challenge you are encountering now on your journey. This could be a financial problem or health problem that you are dealing with.

Give yourself this amount of time to discover the choices of solutions that you might want to choose from. After this period of time, you will be able to see how with each situation you have written, how things will unfold and solutions will come to you.

Don't let this disappointment, problem or challenge have the last word. Work with the tools of flexibility and patience and develop these tools for your toolbox. To have the flexibility to challenge problems and work through them or in some cases, exercise patience and ride out the situation to see if this is leading you in a direction where the outcome might exceed your expectation. Sometimes you will find with patience and not over-reacting the outcome might surprise you and lead to blessings you would not have ever expected.

You will, over time, become adept at the flexibility and creativity of solving problems whether caused by poor choices or circumstances beyond your control.

You will learn that you can expect things to occur in your journey that you were not expecting, but whatever the reason, you will not be a victim of your circumstances; you will be the victor. In looking for a solution to a change in your life or problem, you may discover you have added a tool in your toolbox that you can use as a solution to another problem that you have or something that comes along later in life's journey.

Some of the problems you record may take longer than thirty days to resolve, but what you are doing for the next thirty day period is the exercise of looking for creative solutions for your particular situations.

There may be circumstances where you need professional guidance and that is also another tool, to be able to find the resources you need when you need additional assistance. The same approach applies in tackling the obstacle or challenge and creating your own solution by giving yourself options or getting help to find a solution.

Obstacle in the path of the expectation:	Tools I will use to overcome this obstacle:

Forgive It

TO BE A FORGIVING PERSON is one of the most challenging traits to acquire, but in finding joy in your journey and making the most out of your dash, this is something that will make you or break you.

When saying the Lord's Prayer, for example, the emphasis is being able to forgive others as we hope we will be forgiven.

In today's world, with the violence against people of all ages and heinous acts, how is it even possible to ever succeed at overcoming un-forgiveness?

Forgiving another does not mean that the offending person was not wrong or blameless. However, will holding onto a feeling of resentfulness make the hurt or pain better or reverse the situation so that it never happened? Not possible. Do you think that the offending person is spending any time thinking about how their actions affected you? Not likely. So while you are nursing the offense, the offender is off enjoying their life with no thought as to how their actions have affected you.

As much as possible, remember it will be more beneficial for you in the long run to have a forgiving spirit towards others. Even though you might feel like they deserve retribution and even though they may be wrong and you are in the right. After all, you have been in the same boat and have been the wrong and undeserving person at one time or another.

When someone cuts you off in traffic or rides your bumper, when you clearly have five cars in front of you and no way to go any faster, do your best to choose a forgiving spirit. Even though you are doing what you should be and are in the right and the person behind you is driving dangerously in their impatience and could potentially cause an accident. Take the opportunity in times like this to get into a forgiving mode instead of slamming on the brakes to get even. You might move over and then he can ride the bumper of the car that was in front of you and most likely you will find you have caught up with him at the next red light. It is even more rewarding when because of your forgiving spirit that when the light turns you have actually gotten ahead of him anyway and you have potentially avoided an accident.

If you watch for things like this, when you are in a situation where it would be easy to retaliate – when someone hurts your feelings with their words or has treated you unfairly in any way – to instead, turn the situation around and get in the forgiving mode. You usually come out ahead if you pay attention to the ultimate outcome.

Evaluate the relationships you are in to determine if there is something you can do to make a positive change. In some relationships, even among family members, personalities conflict naturally. If there is conflict, is it possible to minimize the time together. This might prove to be healthier for you.

In cases where people are brought into your life's journey that don't mesh with who you are, move on from including this relationship in your life. Focus on the relationships that are affirming and enriching to your journey. Forgive and let go of the ones that are detrimental.

The approach of rectifying the offense is different from retaliating for the offense. There are ways to rectify the offense in a positive way. One way is by simply moving out of the situation or some other creative way to deal with what is happening and without hanging on to what has happened. It is healthier for you to let it go and move on if possible.

There are two simple ways you can respond to personal questions that might be too personal in nature: "just because" and "for many reasons" and leave it at that.

Unfortunately, strong relationships that you think will last often don't, including marriages of many years. Just as unfortunate is the time wasted in living in a relationship that is over by carrying this person with you into the next phase of your life and continuing to re-live something that has ended.

Instead, determine what can be done to seek out a positive solution to get through the pain of the dissolution of the relationship. In order to move onto where life is taking you, where there could be a tremendous opportunity, staying behind in the past will limit this.

As hard as it is, in the word forGIVE, you have to give to succeed. That is the hard part because why should you give when you feel you have been wronged. In our logical thinking, it does not make sense. However, once you have tried to do this there will be a freeing in your spirit which will make sense because you will be able to let go and move on in your life.

There is no level playing field for the life experience of being a child, and unfortunately, not everyone experiences being fortunate enough to be born into a family with nurturing and caring parents or other family members. The reality is that many have suffered and endured years of abuse – whether physically or verbally -at the hands of their parent or parents or other family members. Something like this can be and needs to be addressed once you are of age and out of that environment.

There is also the life experience of being a child who has lost a loving and nurturing parent at a young age and/or has experienced some other form of trauma or tragedy at a young age.

There are professionals available to you to reach out to for help. To move on through this and to move forward on your journey because now you are in control of your life and you do have options to help you deal with this life experience.

This is part of your dash that cannot be undone, but it can be something that is moved on from so that it does not continue to be a weight that bears down on you throughout the rest of your journey in life. There are people who can help and with the help of people who do care, you can move forward into fulfilling days ahead.

If you cannot let go of the past and carry the past into the present and on into the future, this will limit what you would have experienced because what happened that you won't let go of won't let go of you to enjoy your life.

Replace It

FORGIVE IT AND REPLACE IT go hand in hand. Replace the feelings of wanting to pay back with the alternative choice to forgive and move on.

Envision yourself carrying many rocks around – trying to juggle them all, and making sure that you don't drop any – nursing the offense and what you can do to get even. Can you picture in your mind the burden of carrying large, heavy rocks.

So, while it possibly doesn't make any sense that you should let it go and let the offender off the hook, can you see that it makes perfect sense! Replacing the feelings of anger and resentment and moving to replacing it with forgiveness frees your spirit.

Determine to replace the "rock" of un-forgiveness and envision when you make the choice to forgive that the "rock" is lifted from you tied to a helium balloon that floats away.

When it seems there is no way forgiveness could even be considered, there is no question that in our human reasoning we think why should we? In situations where there is no way to positively rectify the situation, give the situation to God to resolve on your behalf and let go of the spirit of resentment, hostility and the need to get even or to settle the score to pay back for the offense.

Determine to replace the "rock" with a "balloon". Unload yourself of the burden.

Continue to work on replacing the attitude of un-forgiveness in your spirit, by choosing to GIVE a blessing FOR the person. It is like choosing to pick a luscious juicy peach from among the peaches in the bin as opposed to the one which is bruised and rotting.

Are you in an abusive relationship with a partner who demeans you verbally or attacks you physically? Are you in a relationship with a person who influences you to make choices that affect you in a negative way? Can you think of any reason why you would want to have your life restricted and hurting your back from walking around carrying a large "boulder"?

You won't forget what has happened to you, but instead of continuing to carry around what has happened and cannot be undone, GIVE a blessing FOR this person in your spirit. Even though you might think they don't deserve it – you do. You deserve the peace of moving on.

Duplicate the table below. For the next sixty day period, write down the hurts and offenses and how you are choosing to handle this now.

Exercise in Action

Offense	How long did I carry the rock?	When did I let it go and how did I express forgiveness to let go?

By writing down each thing that you perceive as an offense, you will be able to see more clearly if you are being easily offended.

During this exercise you will also clearly see an improvement on how long or if you even carry the "rock". You will get better and better at showing mercy as mercy has been shown to you.

Go back to the list and when you feel that the burden has been lifted off of you and you are free of the burden due to your ability to forgive and leave it behind, throw the list away and move on to enjoy the day you are in and your future.

Control It

I F YOU ARE JUST NOW starting to learn to take charge of your finances and taking on this responsibility that was previously handled by parents, this is a good time in life to begin learning to control spending.

While at university, you may not have things to deal with yet like an electric or water bill if you are residing in a dorm. Often these details are taken care of in the tuition expense. So if this is a time of life right now where income is limited due to being a student, but you are possibly fortunate to also have little financial responsibility, it is still a good time to put into practice controlling the spending on what you do have.

Once money has left your wallet and moved over to wherever you have chosen to send it, it isn't returning to your wallet. So just keep that in mind and put into practice ways of controlling what leaves your wallet to make the most of what you have to use for the needs you will always have.

If you have the opportunity to take a class in money management and investing, take advantage of taking the time now to do this. The investment with what you will learn will pay off.

There are credible financial advisers, who have online courses. You also may find very solid avenues for advice in your local area and within your own university, or even a community college in the area might offer a class.

Also take control to be sure you are putting yourself in the best possible position to move from earning a degree to moving into a career by choosing to focus on a degree that leverages you the best outcome for the best income. Research if going further and pursuing a master's degree or PhD is also going to be a necessity in your field. Art history or opera may be your passion, but be sure there are opportunities for employment that will use your degree in this once you have invested the time and expense to earn the degree.

The culture of today's world is to move your money over to buy their product over a competitor's product and whoever has the most toys wins.

However, that is the culture controlling you instead of your controlling the money you have on hand when you want it and when you need it.

If you live in a space surrounded by the latest in technology from your phone, to your tablet, to your computer, to your big screen television, with the most high end appliances and granite counter tops, but have no money to travel or for other activities because your money is tied up with the necessities of living and the latest gadget on the market, will you be satisfied at the end of your life when all you will be able to do in advanced age is reside in your space with your things. At that point, you may not be seeing what is on the screen of the big screen television or hearing it very well either and at that point your ability to travel may be behind you if the money that would have afforded you opportunities has been used instead for the latest electronic thing.

Even if you have no desire to fly to Europe or China or Sweden or Denmark or Africa, there is a whole country in which you live to explore by car or train and this is especially true if you already live in Europe or Asia because you have access to explore yours and other countries without flying overseas.

So something at this stage of your life to consider because every day you are a consumer.

This is an opportunity to take an exercise to think and come up with strategies that may be useful over the period of your life and depending on what you do, could save you thousands of dollars in waste and turn that money into opportunities for life enriching experiences.

The thought of winning the lottery is appealing because all you have to do is receive money handed to you with no effort other than buying a ticket. If gambling did not work out better for the entity selling the tickets or the casino there would be no gambling. So if you choose to try this route, it's easy enough to keep a record of money you use to gamble - say for a ninety day period - of money out and money in and see who comes out ahead and more often than not, it won't be you.

The names of men and women you know well, in past history and the current age, that have made personal fortunes for themselves are those who have taken risks and made fortunes from their abilities, talents and drive. None are wealthy because they made their money from playing the lottery.

In looking at spending, breaking things down into categories of necessities and wants makes it easier to handle.

If you spend and don't control the wants then you have nothing to use to pay the necessities.

You will have a pretty substantial list of necessities facing you in life. Keeping control and the wants in check, so as not to use money you need for the necessities, will help you have more ultimately for the wants, if you spread the wants out and use your best judgment of when you have the means for the wants.

It also takes persistence and evaluation on your part, but you can also save on the necessities.

One way is to establish and keep a solid credit rating and by controlling spending you should be able to accomplish this.

Having a high credit score can save you money. One example is with a good credit score some utilities allow you to skip paying a deposit up front, where your money is sitting in escrow in their account. By having a high credit score, you are showing financial responsibility.

I also take steps to save on my electric bill by simply incorporating measures to save money in my everyday routine. By not being wasteful, this saves me almost enough money each month to cover the water bill as well. I do the same thing with water usage. Being frugal on these two matters doesn't restrict my use of appliances, air conditioning, running water etc. It is just a matter of using what I need to use and not wasting water and electricity that I don't need to use.

An example of a cost saving step is putting a timer on the water heater so my water heater is only heating the water at the times of day I need hot water and adjusting the thermostat so that my home is not cooled to a comfortable temperature when no one is home to need it that way.

Convenience is another thing that depletes the money you have to use for necessities and wants.

Buying gas and anything from a convenience store will cost you more in most cases.

If you want to make your income go as far as possible, cutting out stops to buy gas or products at a convenience store is a great first step.

It can't be more convenient to have to drive there to pay more for a product than it is to already have the products at home and to have paid much less with planning ahead. That is much more convenient.

It just takes planning to make a list of the things you buy at the convenience store and instead make one trip a month to a store where you know you can get the same products that you want and need at much less cost.

You can set up your own convenience store right in your own home with a little planning and also find the best savings with a little planning and forethought.

You will always pay more for convenience. So just another area you can choose to be in control to save yourself money if you want to turn the tables and keep the money in your wallet to make your money go farther.

Also, take control of making decisions on purchasing that are advantageous to you instead of advantageous to the company's marketing techniques.

There is currently an advertising campaign that wants you to think you have to buy a mattress every eight years because of dead skin cells and dust mites. Mattresses are not an inexpensive item to buy. Most of the recommendations that one needs to replace their mattress frequently comes from mattress manufacturers.

If you do your research and buy a quality mattress that is comfortable for your needs it will be worth the money spent and last for years. The choice of when to replace a mattress is dependent on your comfort and when you feel it needs replacing, not dependent on a marketing campaign to make consumers think they need to go out right now and buy a new mattress. Take control of your spending habits instead of the market place taking control of you.

Take control of your health and weight and work at overcoming anything that is not beneficial to your health and wellbeing. Being informed of healthy choices now will not only benefit you in your twenties and thirties, but on into your eighties and nineties.

Instead of letting your appetite control you, control it. The same situation with convenience stores applies to fast food restaurants that have a product to sell to make a profit and you can contribute to them with your money to help their bottom line and compromise your health or you can take control and find more healthy and less costly alternatives.

Perhaps you are starting to attend a university with access to a fitness center. What an opportunity if this is part of the package and you can use the facility as a student at no expense. Perhaps you are attending a university with access to a pool or a swim team or possibly a sport you haven't yet tried, but you may find in trying out you have a talent for that sport.

Walking is also free. Walking three to five miles is a good aerobic exercise and something you can do on a daily basis. It's as simple as measuring two and a half miles out from your home to walk that distance and back.

You may find yourself at a campus in an area with walking trails in scenic parks or that you are in an area with hiking available in the mountains.

In this like everything else, practice safety and if you feel safer in numbers, find someone or a group to walk together with for a healthful and fun way to exercise.

Exercise in Action

For the next sixty days invest in taking this period of time to really work on focusing each day on spending. Evaluate what you are spending money on and how you can make the money go further by getting the most bang for your buck. Look at your individual pattern of spending and how you can control it. Make your money work for you.

If there is a purchase you plan to make such as a television, laptop etc. instead of going into debt to get it, research products and prices and see if you can save for it by using savings in other areas. Then you aren't overspending. This item has paid for itself in savings. By taking the time to wait and research; you will have a better opportunity to get the best price. You can also research online the best time of year to buy certain products.

Even better than using the savings to buy something that you may not need, would be to invest the savings and watch it grow.

Use this time to explore opportunities that might be available to take a semester course in financial planning and investing and basic health and to explore opportunities on your campus or in your area to start an exercise plan.

Challenge It

C HALLENGE WHATEVER IS IN YOUR life that can be improved upon. Replace regret with responsibility. Responsibility to evaluate the big picture for every situation. What is the potential outcome? Take the time and responsibility to challenge the situation that you are in and then see if there could be negative consequences.

Is speeding to meet a curfew or deadline potentially going to have a tragic outcome for you, your passengers, or another driver? Or, is it better to challenge the first option – speeding – with a better option. Challenge yourself to look at the big picture and not just the immediate need for your self-satisfaction.

Challenge the relationship. Is the relationship that you are in worth going down a path where your potential for success and freedom to achieve (an advanced degree, the freedom and opportunity to enjoy traveling, the opportunity to enjoy and experience and to have the best relationship for you) ended because you didn't challenge it? Consider how relationships could affect the direction of your life.

Envision a bull with a ring through its nose. A powerful animal, now tied to a rope and all it can do is walk around in a circle where it is led day after day. It really goes nowhere except around and around and around in the same circle.

Visualize this as your life. Will temptation control you and lead you easily around and have control of your life or will you Challenge It and control the temptation by evaluating the big picture in every situation because there is an alternative choice in every situation.

Will anger control you or will you control anger. Will greed control you or will you conquer it.

Challenge it with the "five benefits rule". Add this tool to your toolbox so that you are challenging what goes on when necessary so that you have the best outcome for your life.

When you get a cramp or "charlie horse" in your feet or legs, you don't just sit there do you? No, you get up and start moving or walking and the muscles quickly straighten out and the pain subsides. The same principle applies to problems and moving toward a solution when faced with a decision that might be harmful or detrimental to your life and future.

Evaluate habits or behaviors that you have. Evaluate the relationships you are in. Is this the best situation for you at this stage of your life or will it derail the opportunities before you.

Use the five benefits rule to evaluate the temptation, habit or behavior. The five benefits rule is as easy as counting the fingers on one hand. List five benefits if you proceed with the decision. If you cannot come up with a minimum of five benefits – you need to start rethinking and send the idea to the recycle bin.

See in your mind a fan that is closed and envision the fan as one path and this path is not the path that is in your best interest. Whatever the situation you are in, it is like the closed fan going in one direction and on the wrong path. This will never change because this path only goes in one direction.

Now envision opening the fan and thinking of all the prongs as a variety of paths you have to choose from to take that will restore you to a better situation; put you in control instead of your being controlled and get your life on the best path for you.

Challenge it, have high expectations and find solutions to meet your expectations.

Is there a school that you have a desire to attend or a job that you see yourself doing, but you find that there are obstacles in the path to your goal? Replace "I can" and "I can't" with "I'll try". Meaning that maybe you can and maybe you can't, but you won't know until you take the first step and try.

Possibly it will take you out of your comfort zone. Possibly it will require filling out paperwork, securing a loan, moving to a new location. Obstacle after obstacle. Obstacles don't prevent you from trying. They are just obstacles and obstacles can be overcome.

Pray and ask for guidance to "open my eyes to the possibilities and expand my capacity to think and problem solve."

The timing may not be right on the first try, so there can always be a second, third or fourth try.

Do some research on how many tries it took before Thomas Edison had success in his experiments with the light bulb.

To not succeed on the first try is only failure if that is the only try.

Mistakes are part of living and many mistakes will serve a purpose in becoming learning tools that you don't realize at the time you made the mistake. Learn from it and move on. Later, when a similar situation happens, you will remember the previous mistake that may have been very minor, but is now saving you from making a major mistake in another situation.

Take away from your mistake whatever lesson you can learn from the situation instead of spending time regretting that it happened at all. It did happen, but don't waste unnecessary time and energy on regrets over mistakes. Take positive action instead to soothe the sting. The main thing is that the attempt was made. Even if the result was not what you had hoped or expected, you tried, and you can take something away from that. If you watch, you may find that it serves a purpose for you later in a remarkable way that you would not have expected.

Exercise in Action

Use the five benefits rule when a decision or temptation comes up in the day. Write down the situation and list five positives and negatives with continuing to try or quitting.

There might be less drop outs from high school as an example, if they had used the five benefits rule prior to walking away and not finishing high school. It is easy to write five benefits of how staying the course and earning a high school degree will serve you for the rest of your life. It's harder to find five benefits for dropping out.

Try this exercise for a period of sixty days as things come up in your life and keep your lists for future reference to see when it helped you push forward through a tough decision.

Check It

TAKE OUT "THE FEEL" AND replace it with "the real". "Don't be blind; use your mind".

"Don't be blind; use your mind" has useful applications.

Protecting yourself. Protecting and maintaining your property. When making any large purchase (house, appliances, electronics). What you are told by health care professionals related to decisions for your health or if you lose a job (other types of loss).

Protect yourself on your university campus. Don't be oblivious to your surroundings. Don't live under a false sense of security.

Taking the steps necessary to protect yourself is not complicated. Take simple precautions that are sensible and not restrictive like finding a jogging buddy if you jog before dawn. There is better safety in numbers when you are out in the evening as well.

Protect your investments like your vehicle. Take time and check it and verify your understanding of the maintenance required for your particular vehicle. The vehicle will not take care of itself. Understanding when it is necessary to change the oil and how to maintain the tires for safety is simple, and does not take a lot of time. This should be a priority because this is something that is important to you for transportation and your vehicle is an investment that will last if taken care of properly.

When purchasing, check comparable pricing, and also check the opinions and advice you are given by doing your due diligence.

Putting this into practice now, during the time you are at university or going to a vocational school to start your life's career will be an excellent time to gain the experience for larger more expensive purchases as you move on with your journey.

It may make you "feel" great to drive a certain model of car. Don't be "blinded" by the "feeling". Is the car payment or the type of gas needed for this particular model going to suffocate your budget? Check the gas requirements, mileage you will obtain per gallon, maintenance you will have. Are replacement parts reasonable or expensive?

Would you rather go from Point A ……………to……………..Point B with Model ABC…or Challenge It and Check It, and look at Model XYZ that takes you from

Point A………to………………………………….…...Point B – a lot farther than Model ABC because you get better gas mileage, and you are using regular gas instead of premium, your monthly payments are less as well, as is the cost for maintenance, because of the model you have chosen through your research of all of the above.

Double check on information you believe to be true and verify the accuracy. Can you wait and get a better price somewhere else. Is your money really going where you have been told? Do the fees really include all the things you think?

For the next sixty days, check it by duplicating the following table. Put this in an envelope and keep it in a handy location, such as your glove compartment, where it is accessible.

For the next sixty days, before making a purchase that costs over $50.00 – whether the $50.00 is a service or an item - verify the information about what you are getting first before making the purchase. Once you have done this for a period of two months, it will come naturally to you to take the time to verify information to get the best price or hopefully, prevent the opportunity to lose money or be taken advantage of from not understanding or not having all of the facts.

An example would be a store that is advertising a promotion where your purchase for a certain period of time is tax free. That can be a significant savings, so it is tempting to just dive in, but are you really saving this amount or is it really just being hidden in the cost of the item?

The best way to see if this is going to work for you and save you money is to check it and verify it by shopping at least two other locations to compare similar items.

Can you find a better quality item for the same price even after paying the tax? Can you find a better quality item that may even be a bit more, but in the case of a mattress, piece of furniture or appliance, you know is better quality when comparing the two and you know will last longer.

What sounds fantastic may not be so much when you take the time to compare because if you save the tax, but if the product is of poor quality, causes problems and does not last as long as something of better quality, what have you saved?

Also, find out about delivery charges. If you have no tax at one location, but another has a deal on free or reimbursement for delivery charges, and you get the same or better quality, will that be a better deal?

If you go into a store and have a $2.00 off coupon, but it costs you more using the coupon to buy that brand than it would have buying a brand that may have more ounces or is double packed and is comparable, what have you accomplished with your coupon? Using the coupon and only focusing on what you can get with it is really costing you more money.

Look at finding savings when things are very comparable. Consider a newspaper as an example. If there are two Sunday newspapers and one sells for $1.00 and the competitor has their Sunday paper priced at fifty cents, consider what you're getting for the savings. If they both offer what you want, you can spend $52.00 a year, paying $1.00 a week for a newspaper that you're going to read and throw away, or you can pay $26.00 for probably something very comparable. As long as both include what you want, why not save $26.00 and use the savings for a necessity that you need, like lunch money. Savings for things of this type do add up. When you take the time to check it and carry this over to other more costly purchases, you will start getting on the right track and saving money.

If you have developed a company or idea that is making you so much money that $50,000.00 for a car is a drop in the bucket in your income; that is one thing. However, most are being deceived by the perceived status inherent in driving a certain brand of car, when really, as long as it has four tires and a motor and is comfortable for you, you and the luxury car driver will get to the same destination. However, the other driver will likely pay a much higher price than you will to get there, over time, considering increased insurance premiums, low mileage per gallon, and higher gas prices due to having to use premium gas, and more expensive maintenance because the parts will cost more.

The other thing that most are deceived on is the waste that comes with only using the product two or three years and then getting a new product, which wastes more of your income. Instead, it would be wiser to buy quality products that will last and be economical to maintain, while banking and saving the money spent to replace something in a couple of years.

Also, with any advice or information you receive, it is important to check it not only with your finances, but also with advice you are given related to your health.

If you receive advice that you need to have a root canal for example, it could be advisable to have a second opinion to be sure that is the only treatment option.

It is important to take the time to check it, to verify the advice you are given whether it is medical or financial. The outcome can be detrimental or beneficial when you are being given medical or financial advice so it is always advisable to protect yourself in all situations and check it.

The following exercise will help you with evaluating and checking it whether with information, advice or money.

After a two month period, evaluate the notes and comparisons that you have made over the period of time. This will be a more fun exercise if you have the time to just shop and compare prices and don't really need the items right now. That way you can really compare lots of things with no intention of purchasing now, and just to have the time to explore, take notes, catch onto the gimmicks. With this experience, when your washing machine really does fail and you have to buy a replacement in a hurry, you will have the tools in your tool box to make the best decision because you have done a run through when you didn't have the pressure of having to make an immediate purchase.

You will find in reviewing your notes, that by taking the time to research and verify and check it, you have realized a significant savings.

Exercise in Action

What I want to purchase?	Research used	Result
What was I told and is it correct?	What did I do to check it	Result

Find It

IF YOUR PET RAN AWAY, you would make every attempt to recover your lost pet. You wouldn't just stand at the front door and call the pet's name would you? You would call neighbors to see if they might have seen your pet, post flyers, call the animal shelter, get in your car and drive and walk the area trying to locate your pet and bring it back home safely.

Sometimes, the pet just shows up, but not always. So you apply the "Find It" technique on any loss that is not final (like a car wrecked or something destroyed beyond repair).

A job loss or any missed opportunity is not final unless you perceive it to be. You won't perceive it to be if you remember your next step is to "find it".

Although you want to find your same pet that you lost, you can't do that with a job loss or opportunity missed. So you will focus on finding the next job and the next opportunity with the same focus and determination you would if it were a lost pet.

You are not happy that the job is lost, but fortunately for you, it is just a job and not your beloved pet who is one of a kind. It's true that while your pet is the best, and you find it hard to think you could ever find another pet you would love as much, in this case, you now have the chance to possibly find a better job and one that you will love even better than the one you lost. You may even come away with a higher income and better benefits. But you have to "find it". It is not going to find you. Just as you would use creativity to find something that is lost, you need to do the same with recovering in a job loss or loss in a personal relationship.

If there was a contest telling you that there was money to be found, but it would take solving clues to discover where the money was, you would be using your mental resources to solve the clues to discover the location of the money and take home the prize.

The same holds true for moving forward with your solution for the loss of a personal relationship or job. It will take effort on your part with problem solving and creating solutions. You need to take control of the circumstances. The circumstance should not take control of you. Anger, bitterness, crying over spilt milk over the loss of a relationship or job, not getting the promotion or job you expected, is letting the circumstance control you. Whereas, developing a plan to overcome the loss is taking the circumstance and gaining control over it.

Whenever you experience the emotion of disappointment or loss or that something has changed that you were not expecting instead of focusing on that, look forward to the next opportunity.

When you drive, you use the rearview mirror to be sure you are safe when backing up, but in order to get to your destination you look and focus on moving forward. You don't go backwards. Leaving the past behind and looking forward to what is ahead is what should be your focus.

There have been many tragic situations with suicide where a circumstance took control and a person did not try to find it. Ending their life, there is no second act. In finding it, the success after the disappointment or trial might have outshone what had at first been a loss. Often this is the case, that more positive results can develop after what seems to be a loss.

It is devastating to see people lose their homes as the result of floods, fires, tornadoes or hurricanes. It is devastating to see farmers lose their crops as a result of drought or for many other reasons, but farmers are an example of awesome problem solvers who deal with the trials and changes that affect them and rise to the occasion to move forward with solutions; to find it.

The exercise for the next four month period is to discern areas where you feel that goals were not achieved that you had expected or if you have a loss of some kind that you are dealing with. A loss might just be a setback and you might have to take an alternate path on the road on your journey to get back to the main road of where you want to be. Reach into your tool box for resources from what you have put there from the previous exercises. Put in all the effort and creativity you can to look for ways to find it in your situation.

Exercise in Action

Trial or loss I am dealing with	Alternate goal	Steps to take to accomplish this

Enrich It

T AKE TIME TO REPLENISH YOUR spirit. There is time wasted that you will never recoup and there is time well spent. Learning something new, or expanding your knowledge base about something you already have experience with, is time well spent, as is the time you spend to replenish your spirit as well.

Whether or not you already have a belief or faith, this is an opportunity to take a brief period of time to become further informed and educated outside of the classroom.

For a twelve-week period, commit to one hour of your time each week to community worship. That equates to not much more than twelve hours of your time in a three month period.

Think of this as an additional elective for your classes for a semester where you can learn and stretch your knowledge and experience.

Most of the classes you will take at university are one hour to an hour and a half in length for a class period, so this is not taking any more time in the day than your regular class. This will give you an ample opportunity to observe and explore and this exercise will either end after three months or be a beginning.

When spending an hour or more a night watching the news or a show on television, three or more hours on the computer, or watching sports or a movie, you can see how small a commitment this is. Particularly when you know of people who will stand in line for an hour or more to purchase a new electronic item or tickets to a concert or sit out in the rain or freezing weather to watch a sporting event. You have to do none of this to join a worship service.

In addition to being a small percentage of time compared to the time spent on things like walking the mall and the examples above, the other difference is that this hour is not about your entertainment.

The point is the ability you have to turn the tables from self to something more than self. It opens you up to learn and expand your knowledge and experience - for a minimal amount of time – approximately one hour a week.

Focus on what you will learn and take with you to use on your life's path, rather than presumptions on "religion". Broaden your foundation, rather than focusing on what others say or have said. This will give you a fresh opportunity to build only the relationship and connection that is unique to you as an individual.

Whether you have a faith based experience from childhood or you do not, think of it as doing a research project. Research four or five places of worship nearby and commit to attend one each Sunday for the next month.

This can be an enriching project no matter whether you are attending university in a new town where everything is unfamiliar to you, or if you are in the area you have lived your whole life. You may be living or going to university in a college town with a historical church in the area and what an opportunity to experience this while you are in this life experience.

Take notes. Learn and take away from the experience as much as you can. Be receptive to meeting strangers. Take the initiative and introduce yourself – you may foster another relationship that might help you in your present situation at the university you attend, in your career path, or in your current job.

The remaining two months do the same so that by the end of the three-month period you have visited twelve separate places of worship. You may also choose to invite a fellow classmate or co-worker or several friends to join you in this and this might enrich your experience even more.

At the end of the three-month period, evaluate the information that you have gotten from the experience and then decide if you wish to continue.

Possibly if you are attending university in a town far from home one of the places of worship could be somewhere you would enjoy continuing to attend for the time you are in school there and well might enhance your university experience since this is a brief chapter in your life. Even though the time you are in university is brief, it is important as a springboard for your future.

It will be interesting to observe after each Sunday, if what you hear and learn influences decisions that you make for the rest of the week. Are there situations that you look at with a different perspective than before just from being in a different environment and having this experience that again is unique to your journey?

Just as being informed about the steps you need to take to get the most out of the investment you put in the vehicle you drive, this twelve-week experience might provide you with information that will benefit you in your journey through life. The decision about what you do, or don't do, with the information, is yours. Building a relationship with God is an individual matter, and not something based on the opinions of others or something you might have previously heard. Give yourself the opportunity to explore this relationship as an open minded individual; disregarding what outside influences or opinions you may previously have heard.

Exercise in Action

Using the planner below, set up an itinerary for the next three months as you would plan for the schedule of one of your classes. Stretch yourself in this experience and enjoy!

Date:	Location/Time:
1.	
2.	
3.	
4.	
5.	
6.	
7.	
8.	
9.	
10.	
11.	
12.	
	Look back and what do you know now that you might use on life's journey that you did not know at week one

Return It

T HERE IS A CHOICE FOR everyone to be either a giver or a taker in moving along the journey of life. There is a choice for everyone to share the light of your life and spread your brightness to others, but only the individual person has the power of choice in this matter to do this.

On almost a daily basis on the news, there are examples of persons who are takers and who have given into the temptation of Evil and their pride to make the choice to follow, instead of to choose to use their intellect and power of control to choose a different way.

There is giving from your spirit and giving from your resources so this is a short sixty day exercise in the power of and blessing of being a giver in two ways – spiritual and financial – to experience both.

There are nine fruits of the spirit: Love, joy, peace, patience, kindness, goodness, faithfulness, gentleness, and self-control.

Combine self-control/goodness and faithfulness/gentleness. Research for yourself each fruit of the spirit listed.

Using the chart below for a two month period focus on one fruit of the spirit each day and observe if anything happens in your day where you notice this attribute in your interactions with others.

During the same sixty day period, tithe ten percent of the gross of what you receive during each pay period during this time. You can see when you put this in perspective, this is not a percentage that is unreasonable to give looking at the visual below and what you have left – the 90%.

$ - 10% Tithe	$$$$$$$$$$- 90% for you

Many people tithe at their regular place of worship. If you do not have a regular place of worship, find a ministry or outreach program at a place of worship that you can support, and give your gift to them or research and give to a charity.

Many places of worship have programs to help the homeless, or they may have Meals on Wheels or a similar program which assists persons who are elderly and/or homebound with their meals.

Tithing for many is difficult because it is hard to let go. Hold your hands palm side up in front of you and make a fist and this is how many feel about their money and giving. However, in this posture, you also cannot receive anything.

Now open your hands and you are in a posture of giving and receiving.

The purpose here for giving in the sixty day period is for you to find what you experience with the exercise, both spiritually and financially.

You already know from previous chapters how to control it and not waste your 90% and to look for wise investments. You will now experience, if you pay attention, that you will come across unexpected savings in the posture of giving, and for many reasons you will come out ahead as will the beneficiaries of your generosity.

Exercise in Action

	Fruit of the Spirit	10% of gross - tithe per pay check
Mon	faithfulness/gentleness	
Tues	self-control/goodness	
Wed	love	
Thurs	joy	
Fri	peace	
Sat	patience	
Sun	kindness	

Imagine It

INSTEAD OF MAKING A RESOLUTION, at the beginning of the new year, imagine it, and develop goals instead. Each January, think of three goals you would like to accomplish in the next twelve months, one goal to accomplish in the next three years, one goal in the next five years.

For the next assignment, complete the following document and then do this every year during the month of January to create three new goals to accomplish in that year, one new three year goal, and one new five year goal.

The list can be as varied as your imagination; with things that interest you and that you would like to accomplish.

Examples: Reading a particular classic novel that you have always wanted to read in the next year; visiting a local historical place of interest near your campus on a weekend; save for the next three years to be able to take advantage of a semester abroad if that is offered at your university; save for a cruise to Alaska for your five year goal as part of celebrating graduation. Don't leave off goals that seem unrealistic or impossible.

Include them and watch for opportunities to present themselves to achieve those goals.

Some goals you may have to plan to have enough money saved to accomplish the goal, and others won't cost anything.

Maybe you have always wanted to learn to play a particular instrument. Starting lessons could be a new goal for the year. You might be able to take lessons off campus or you might find someone on campus who is willing to teach you at less cost.

As you work toward these goals, don't let discouragement creep in if some of the goals get sidetracked unexpectedly. Delays may work out to your advantage; time will tell. Goals deferred does not mean failure. The only failure is never starting.

Focus on the goal and a realistic timeframe. Don't let age, money or any other distraction figure into it when you imagine your goal list.

Some goals may include the time needed to save the money to use to make the goal happen. Again, this is not putting off the goal; you are just figuring into the time frame a period of time to save, which is part of the equation.

Part of looking for opportunities during this saving period would be opportunities to fund raise, as well as save. Opportunities to tweak expenses, discover opportunities for making money you may not have thought of before. Are you exceptionally good in a subject. Could you tutor for a short period of time to make extra cash.

Don't be put off by obstacles or perceived challenges.

Have you ever been stopped in traffic on the interstate and noticed weeds, grass or vines appearing in the cracks of the interstate structure? How did those plants penetrate the hard concrete and how does it continue to grow and thrive in that environment. There is not potting soil for the roots, no flower bed, no one nurturing or taking care of it. Yet, unless the road crew comes along and digs it or pulls it out, it continues to grow and thrive in an unlikely and hostile environment.

The same can happen with your dreams and the goals you set for yourself.

The seed from which the vine, flower, or weed grew in the first place in the crack in the concrete doesn't think logically that it should not be able to even get started in that environment. This is not tilled soil on a farm where a seed should get its start. This is a structure that's function is to support heavy vehicles; not provide a place for nature to show its resilience. But nature will not be controlled and your dreams will not be controlled and restricted if you don't allow it.

Even if the goal is not realized for some reason the way you feel it should have been, there may be a better opportunity that is just over the next hill. But if you put the brakes on, you will never get to the next hill to see what opportunity there was.

Often, the runner up of the race might find that his opportunity in the long run turns out to better than the one afforded to the winner of the race. However, if the runner up is so focused on the fact that he did not come out the winner and therefore only perceives second, third or whatever place, as being in a losing position, then ultimately, it will be a losing position.

What positive outcome can there be in taking on the role of the sore loser? Instead, focus on the possibilities of what could be building from the position you are in and what you have to bring to the table.

Just because one talk show host is rated number one, does that mean you only watch that program? Or, do you decide which talk show host you like and which show you want to watch. How many radio stations do you listen to that claim that they are rated number one? Almost all of them, but that is not why you choose the station. You choose what you like. Same goes for what happens when you find yourself overlooked for a promotion, or reward, etc. Look for other opportunities; look for divine clues and guidance, and show patience. The wait may be well worth it and the outcome may be much better.

If you are afraid, start working on the goal even if you are in the emotion of fear while you're doing it. Don't let fear sidetrack you. When fear knocks on the door, send faith and courage to answer it.

Exercise in Action

Goals written: January _____	
one year goals	date accomplished
1.	
2.	
3.	
three year goal	date accomplished
1.	
five year goal	date accomplished
1.	

Enjoy It

I N THE COURSE OF TAKING care of daily responsibilities, don't overlook your surroundings and what you can add to the day, week, or situation to make it enjoyable.

If you're embarking on your first year of college, or have moved to a new location to start a job after high school, evaluate your surroundings. Are there opportunities to volunteer on campus, join clubs, tutor fellow students, or take on a part-time job in the community in between classes or on weekends.

Although your first priority is devoting the time needed for you classes and studies also make time to enjoy the experience.

If you've landed your first job since graduating from high school, try to learn as much as possible about the culture of the company you are working for. Build relationships. Research what other activities the company might be involved in such as a charity event or sponsoring a sports team.

If you find that you are in a new location after graduating from high school or college, do research on the area. Even if, for a while, you are doing this by yourself, spend time experiencing the area in which you live and see what is available to you in your new environment.

In some careers, in order to advance, one has to be flexible and willing to move to another location where the opportunity is, and this can be a challenge at the start. If this moves you to a better place on your career path, then while it might take you out of your comfort zone initially, look for ways you can enjoy where you land for the time you are there.

I had a friend tell me that he and his wife always tried to bloom where they were planted in the many moves throughout his military career. Wherever they were relocated and didn't have any friends or family, they made new friends and made the most of the new experience.

In your twenties, starting your career, you may be able to additionally handle a part-time job which could give you the opportunity not only to work in an area that interests you, but also provides you extra income to meet a goal, such as saving to have a fund for vacations or to earmark that money totally toward investing for a retirement nest egg. This is a great idea since the earlier you start the better. If you can handle it even for just a year or two, having a part-time job on top of your full time career and banking all the money from the part-time job towards savings and investing is a great foundation to have. There are many opportunities for part-time work.

If this works out and you can handle it with your other responsibilities, you might find an experience you will enjoy that you have never tried before. You might explore something that you don't want to do as a full time career, but still have a skill for. As an example, you might become licensed in therapeutic massage therapy and work a few hours in the evening during the week or perhaps one Saturday a month. Perhaps you grew up with a parent who taught you carpentry skills throughout your life and you have a talent that you can use so you decide to become a licensed contractor to be able to take on home repair jobs when time allows. This allows you to use your interests and abilities to bring in a good amount of additional income on top of your full time income and reap the benefits by enjoying the fruits of your labor either in additional money to put toward a good retirement fund or a fully paid vacation without going into debt.

You might live in a state where there are many theme parks and you have a talent and enjoyment for dancing or singing and performing. You may consider working a couple of nights or weekends performing and doing something you enjoy and also having a second income.

You may have grown up in a household where you were taught skills from a parent such as baking or repairing the family car. You may be adept at plumbing. There might be opportunities at local hotels for part-time work where your skills could be used to get extra income after your full time job.

If you are in a position to do this, before life moves on to the stage of marriage and starting a family, where you can work extra hours and family time with a spouse and children is not affected, these years are good years to consider the opportunity of a second income. This will no doubt help down the road having that extra financial stability, and could also be something to fall back on should you ever be laid off in your full time job.

Whether you are working or attending university away from home or in the town you have lived in all of your life, take advantage of exploring all of the leisure opportunities in the area in which you live so that you are enjoying that environment while you are there, since transfers can happen or you may move to a new area after graduation. Make the memories and enjoy what is around you in your special area now.

Use caution and your judgment when you find yourself in situations where the behavior and what is happening around you is questionable. This is when the five benefits rule will come in handy to determine if it would be more beneficial to remove yourself from what is happening at the party or function.

Exercise in Action

Use the following exercise to look at opportunities available in your environment that you would enjoy. Perhaps you are in an area of the country with mountains and you have never hiked or snow skied in the winter. For the next two months, take a few minutes each week to fill in a chart like the one below to make notes of new experiences in your area to enjoy.

Environment (school, job, city)	Opportunities within the environment

Relish It

CONGRATULATIONS TO YOU IF YOU did persevere and maybe high school was not a breeze for you, but you stayed the course and earned your degree and now you are moving on with your life's adventure with this milestone accomplished.

Not everyone finds sitting in classrooms taking courses they find no purpose in and taking tests tolerable; so congratulations for not giving up and not giving in to the feelings to quit before making it to graduation and earning your high school degree. Well done.

Your high school degree is important to moving into your future and now that you have accomplished this milestone in life you are ready to move on to continue to grow and learn in life.

Everyone has strengths and weaknesses. Not everyone is successful in an academic setting.

When you move on from high school to find the field where you can use your interests and strengths you will experience a sense of accomplishment.

Find your passion and find your career where you can live your passion through your work. Strive to find a career where you can be self-sustaining even if eventually you have a spouse. It is important to have the ability of have an income independently to cover and protect yourself.

Congratulations to those who are high academic achievers; who have taken advantage of the opportunity to take advanced courses and are moving out into the world to take on even more challenges.

Whether your time in school was one with high academic achievements or not, now you have the opportunity to use the other strengths and talents that you have other than academic success that are important as well.

Now your goal is to develop the tools that you are acquiring on your journey and putting in your tool box to use as needed. To relish it for what you will contribute and accomplish in life.

It won't seem long before you are getting an invitation for your ten year high school class reunion. So whether you are just now headed toward that milestone or past that milestone, for wherever you are, relish the day that you are in.

If you had to leave high school for some reason or could not go to college, but are now in a position that you can reconsider these opportunities, don't ever think it is too late to start again to secure your degree.

This might be the time when you are in a position to know more about career opportunities that will use your particular talents and strengths and where to go to get the best schooling and training for that opportunity.

Take advantage of the experience you do have and don't be afraid to stretch yourself and even move into exploring a different career path if you feel lead to do so no matter what your age.

For those who choose a career path into one of the branches of the military right from graduation from high school, after a twenty year career, there are still many years ahead to explore and use the advantages of the discipline and training learned in a career with the military to move into another career path.

There is no do-over to go back and fix the day before. So look for and relish the blessings of the present day to take advantage of what is happening right now in this day. Go forward to find the next school or career move that you feel is best for you and relish it when you succeed.

Of course, there will be bad days – even possibly tragic days. You will experience the loss of family members and friends. You may experience financial loss. If you find that your path takes you into a minefield instead of a meadow, make the effort to take the steps to continue to move forward on the path, over the bridge, through and out of the minefield, to find the next meadow.

Circumstances will happen, but circumstances can change or be changed or worked through. Solutions have to be looked for; they don't usually fall in your lap.

The difference is you know now how to forgive, how to nurture relationships, how to look at the situations and problems that come up along your path and tunnel under them or find an alternate path around them. Difficulties won't defeat you because you know that you will continue to persevere and eventually you will find a solution.

Relish the successes that happen because of your efforts and the blessings that come your way. If you learned something from an unpleasant situation or problem that you can use moving forward, that is definitely something to relish.

Look for clues for God's guidance and purpose for your life and you are well on your way to finding meaning in your dash. Today is the day to have the time of your life. Use the tools you have put in your toolbox along the way; relish it and find your joy in your journey.